I AM A PROUD INDIAN

Coloring Book Indian

JUPITER KIDS

JUPITER KIDS
CHILDREN'S & KIDS FICTION

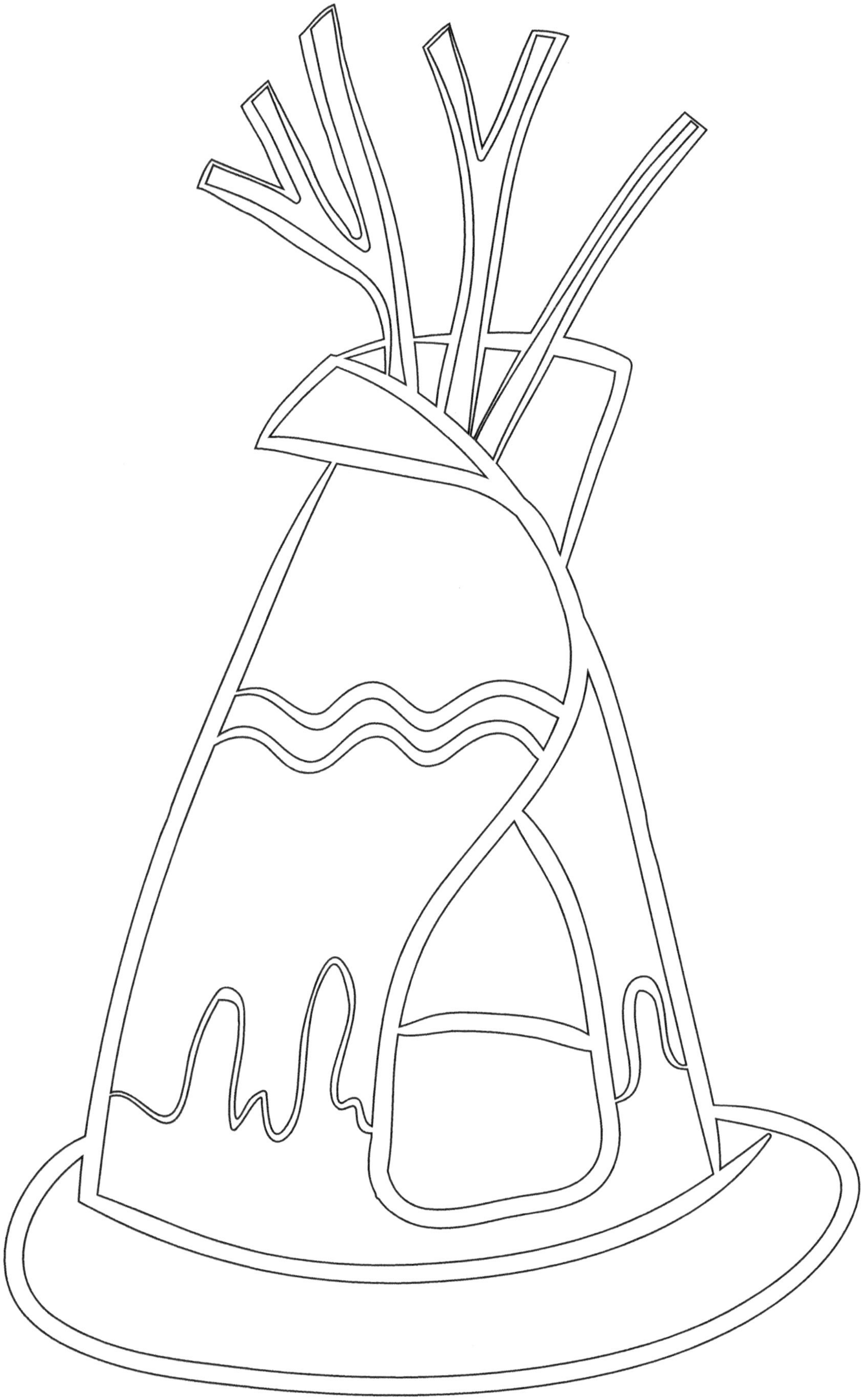

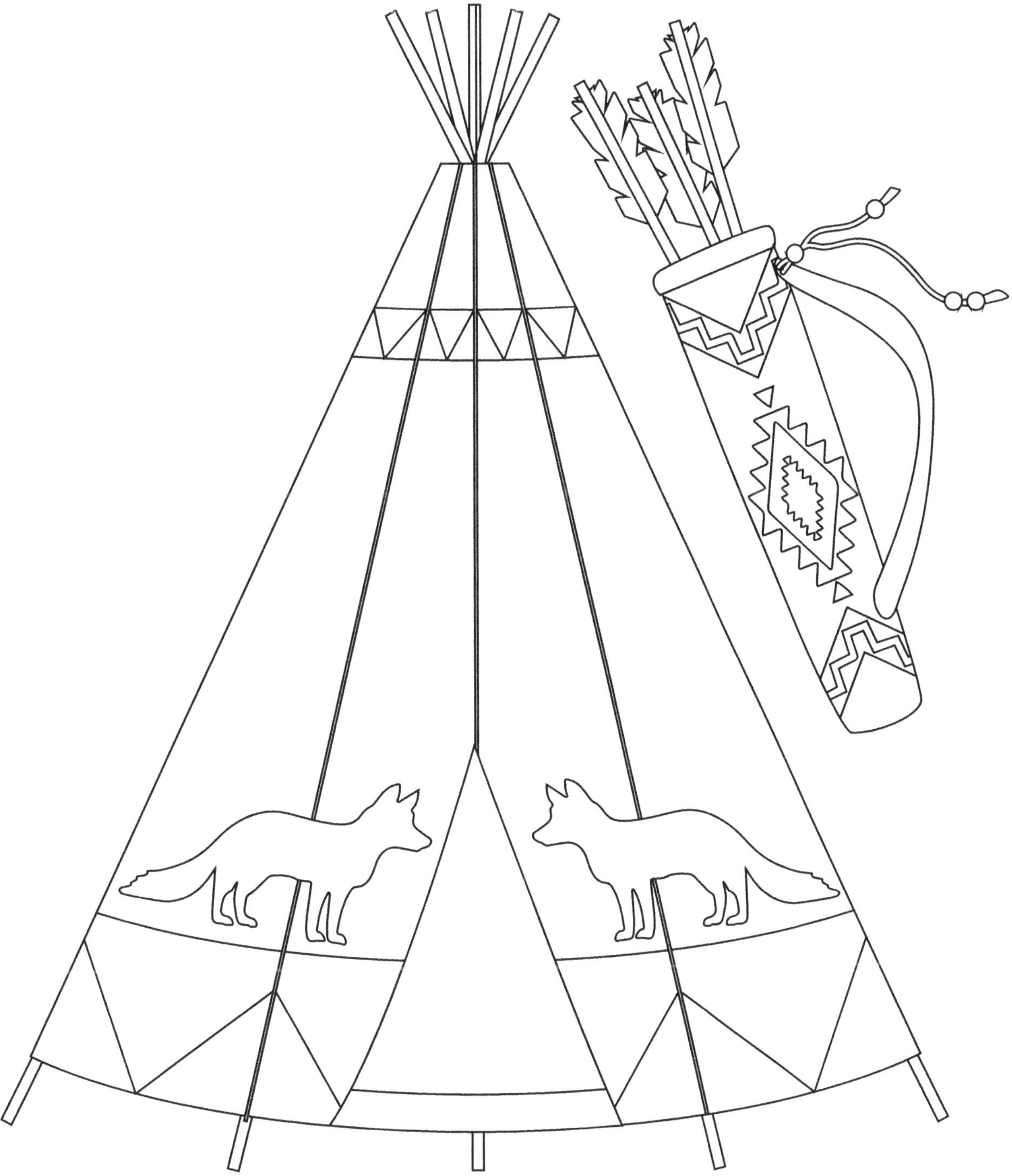

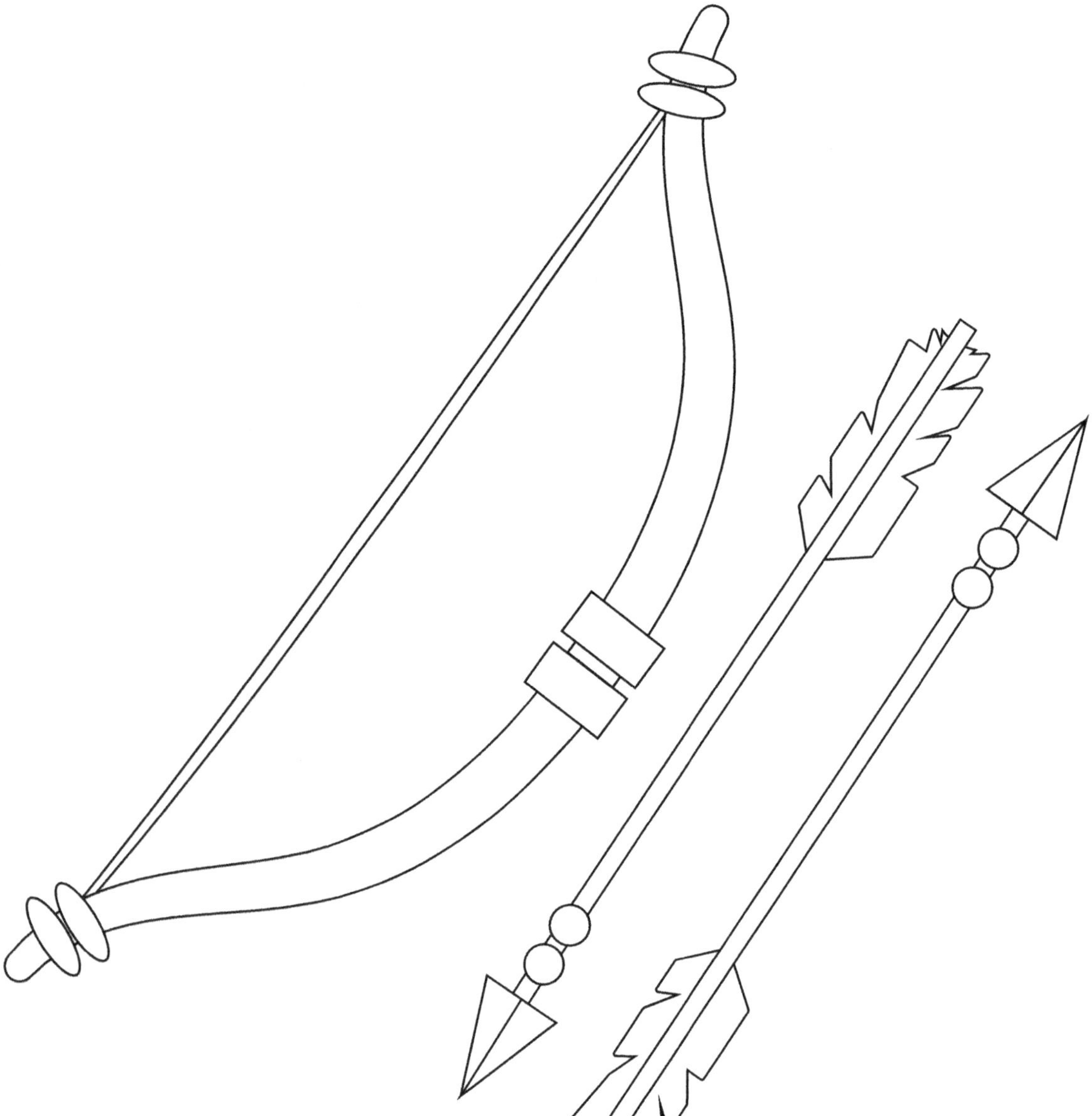

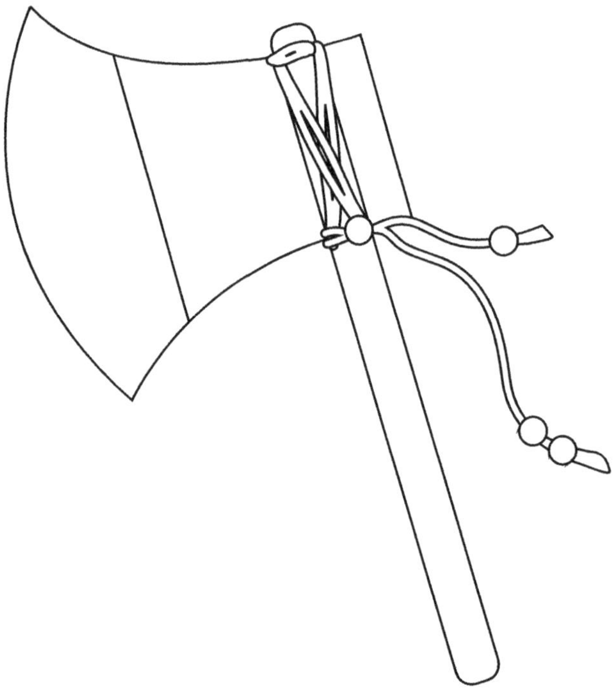

Continue the fun.
Color these totem
poles next!

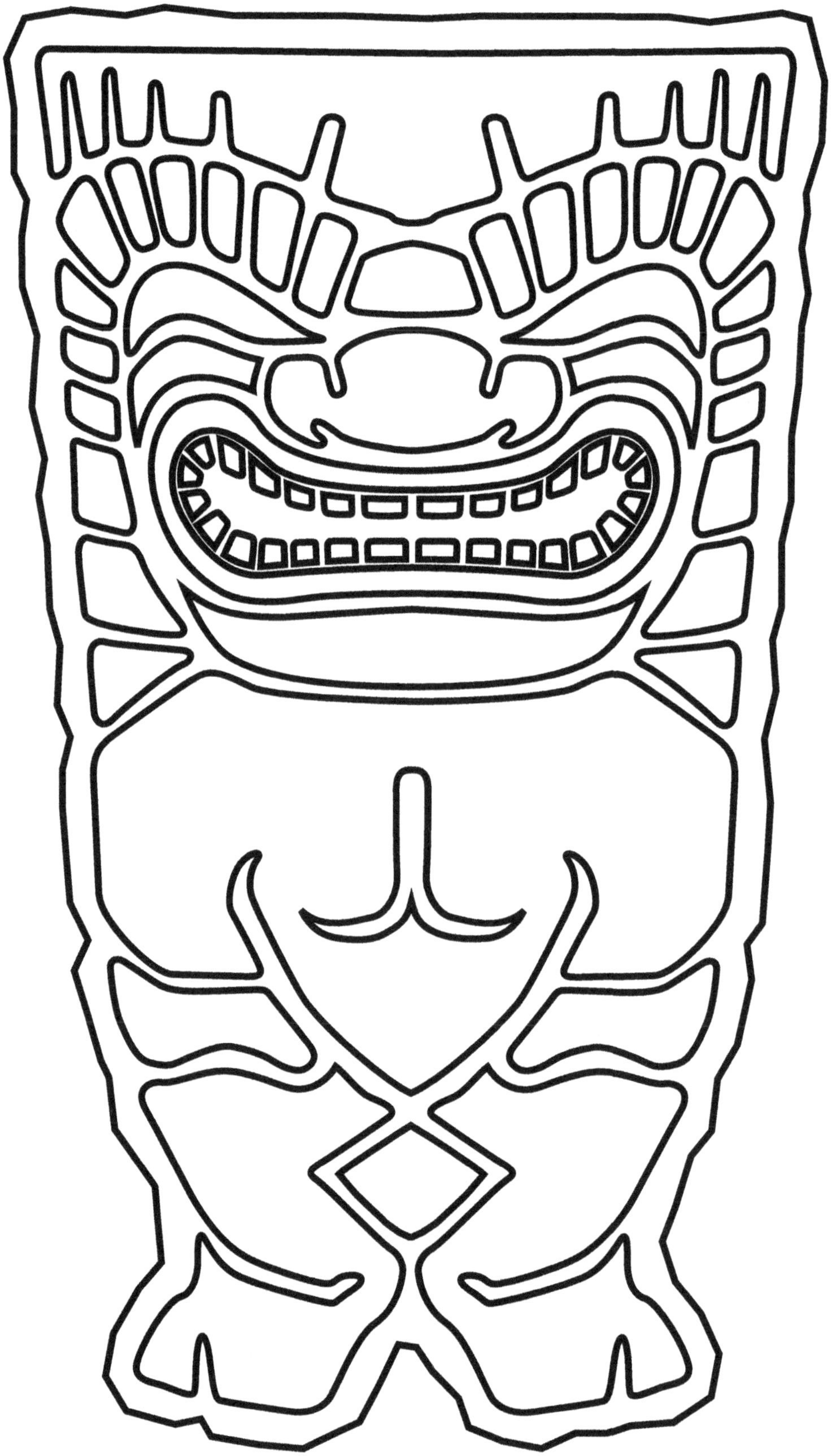

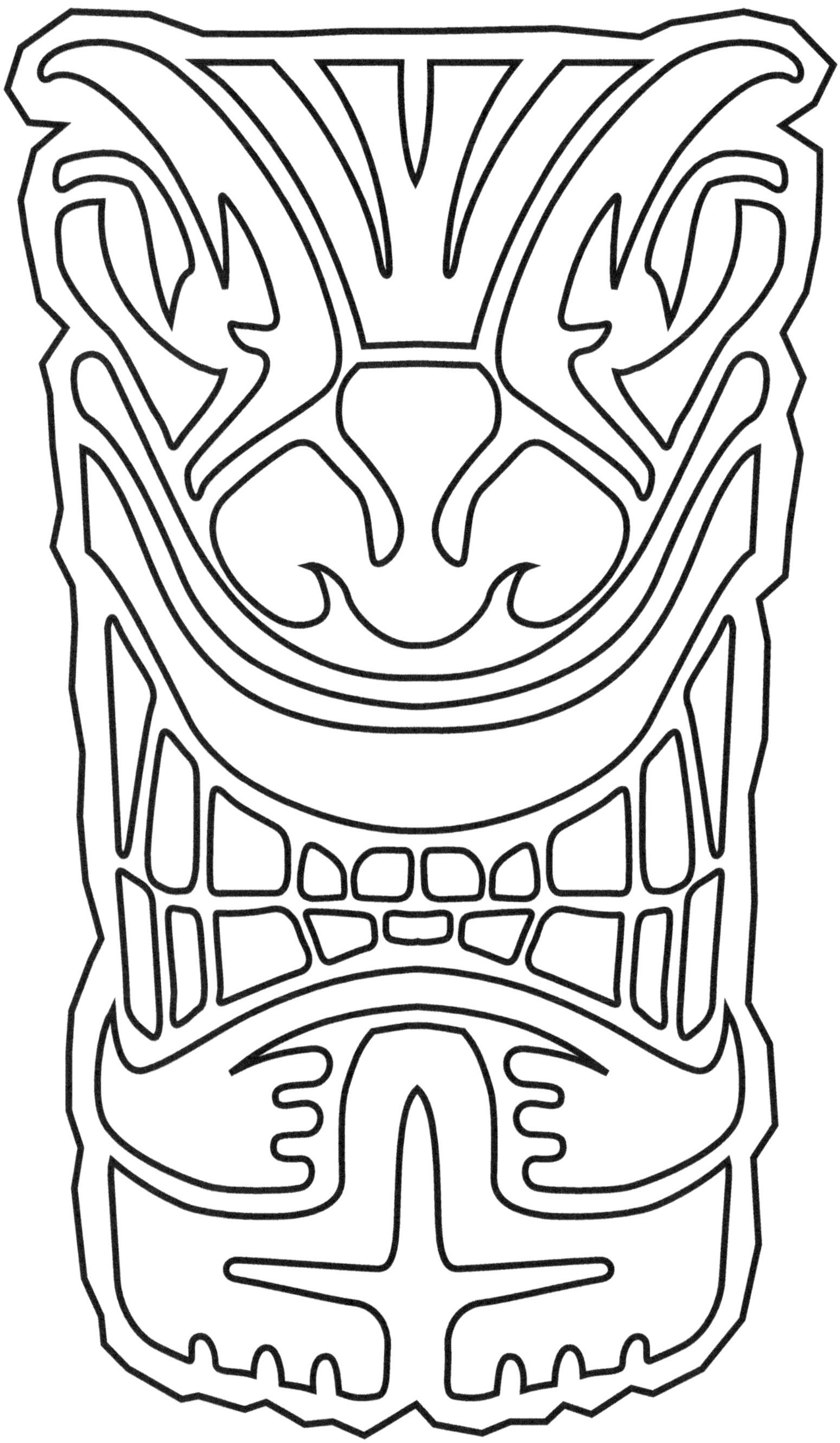

Made in the USA
Las Vegas, NV
08 May 2021

22600547R00059